D0119333

Aberdeenshire Library and Information Service
www.aberdeenshire.gov.uk/alis
Renewals Hotline 01224 661511

- 2 JUL 2013
- 3 AUG 2013
24 SEP 2013
17 Oct 2013
- 9 NOV 2013
15 SEP 2014
27 NOV 2017

ABERDEENSHIRE LIBRARIES WITHDRAWN FROM LIBRARY

GIFFORD, Clive

Millionaires

ALIS
2599152

weblinks

You don't need a computer to use this book. But, for readers who do have access to the Internet, the book provides links to recommended websites which offer additional information and resources on the subject.

You will find weblinks boxes like this on some pages of the book.

> **weblinks**
>
> For more information about Jamie Oliver, go to www.waylinks.co.uk/21CentLives/Millionaires

waylinks.co.uk

To help you find the recommended websites easily and quickly, weblinks are provided on our own website, **waylinks.co.uk**. These take you straight to the relevant websites and save you typing in the Internet address yourself.

Internet safety

- Never give out personal details, which include: your name, address, school, telephone number, email address, password and mobile number.
- Do not respond to messages which make you feel uncomfortable – tell an adult.
- Do not arrange to meet in person someone you have met on the Internet.
- Never send your picture or anything else to an online friend without a parent's or teacher's permission.
- If you see anything that worries you, tell an adult.

A note to adults
Internet use by children should be supervised. We recommend that you install filtering software which blocks unsuitable material.

Website content

The weblinks for this book are checked and updated regularly. However, because of the nature of the Internet, the content of a website may change at any time, or a website may close down without notice. While the Publishers regret any inconvenience this may cause readers, they cannot be responsible for the content of any website other than their own.

WAYLAND

21st CENTURY LIVES
MILLIONAIRES

Clive Gifford

WAYLAND

First published in 2007 by Wayland

Copyright © Wayland 2007

Wayland
338 Euston Road
London NW1 3BH

Wayland
Hachette Children's Books
Level 17/207 Kent Street
Sydney, NSW 2000

All rights reserved

British Library Cataloguing in Publication Data
Gifford, Clive
Millionaires. – (21st century lives)
1. Millionaires – Biography – Juvenile literature
I. Title
305.5'234'0922

ISBN: 9780750250429

Printed in China

Wayland is a division of Hachette Children's Books.

ABERDEENSHIRE LIBRARY AND INFORMATION SERVICES	
2599152	
HJ	598011
J920	£11.99
JU	PORP

Cover: Jamie Oliver in his London restaurant, Fifteen.

The publishers would like to thank the following for permission to reproduce their pictures:
Cover and 20 Rex Features; 4 Jim Winslet, Newscast; 5 Schoolsnet; 6 Dave M. Bennett, Getty Images; 7 AFP, Getty Images; 8 Stephen Hird, Corbis; 9 Gregory Heisler for *Time*, Corbis; 10 and 11 Ajaz Ahmed; 12 Seth Wenig, Corbis; 13 AFP, Getty; 14 Chris Jackson, Getty; 15 Rune Hellestad, Corbis; 16 Kimberly White, Corbis; 17, Walt Disney Pictures/Pixar Animation, Corbis; 18 Andreau Daimau, Corbis; 19 David Willis, Alamy; 21 Peter Dench, Corbis.

Contents

Tom Hadfield

Website Whizzkid

Tom Hadfield, founder of Soccernet and General Manager of Schoolsnet.

"It just happened – neither of the companies were planned. When I was twelve I was putting football scores on the Internet as a hobby, and as it happened this turned out to have commercial potential. Both my Dad and I have had to learn as we went along since neither of us have any experience in setting up businesses."

Startup Spotlight ZDNet UK, April 2000

Name: Thomas David Hadfield

Year and place of birth:
1982, Wakefield, UK

Education: Tom went to Dorothy Stringer High School and took his A-Levels at Varndean Sixth Form College. He is currently studying at the prestigious Harvard University in the United States, majoring in government in the class of 2008.

Career highs: Tom founded the first commercial football website, Soccernet. The website was sold in 1999 for approximately £25 million. In 2001, still in his teens, he was honoured as a 'Global Leader of Tomorrow' by the World Economic Forum. At 19, he was the youngest person ever to win the award.

Away from work: Tom is a keen environmental activist. He has been involved in many projects to improve access to clean drinking water around the world.

Something you might not know about him: Tom is no unfit computer geek. He is a keen football goalkeeper and was at English professional team Brighton and Hove Albion's Centre of Excellence from under-11 level through to the under-16s. At the age of 17, while developing his second Internet start-up project, he was Sussex County Schools' goalkeeper.

Make a million: Tom Hadfield spotted a gap in the market and went for it. He quickly latched on to how many soccer-mad Internet surfers wanted up-to-the-minute live football scores and results, and worked hard to provide a solution. Throughout this hectic time, he kept up his education and stayed in touch with his friends. This has helped him on future projects.

It all started round at Rupert's house. Twelve-year-old Tom Hadfield's friend had Internet access, a rare thing in Britain in 1994. Tom, who had been fascinated by computers since he was very young, was hooked on the Internet. There, he discovered that people in other parts of the world followed English football but had to wait days for the newspapers carrying the results to arrive.

With Internet access at home by the end of 1994, Tom figured out a way of putting up all the football results online so that people could have access to them. At 3pm on 19 August 1995, the opening day of the new Premiership season, the Soccernet website went live. At first, there were just a few people visiting the website each day, but this number grew into hundreds and thousands within the first year. The company that his father worked for, Associated Newspapers, began to invest in the site. For Euro '96, Tom struck his first major deal with Yahoo! worth £40,000. He was still only 13.

If Euro '96 made Soccernet, it was the 1998 World Cup which saw the company truly boom. During the four-week tournament, Soccernet was attracting 300,000 users per day. The company sold £1.5 million of advertising during the World Cup. This made it one of the most successful sports websites of the time. Soccernet's success attracted potential buyers. In June 1999, American cable TV network ESPN paid £25 million for the company.

Tom didn't believe in standing still and at the height of Soccernet's success, he was already planning his next Internet company. Schoolsnet was launched in 1999 offering a complete revision and tips database for schoolchildren, as well as advertising teaching jobs and school supplies.

The level of media interest in teenage businessman Tom during this time was extraordinary. He was featured in *Vanity Fair* and *Time* magazines, all the UK national newspapers and met with British government officials at the Prime Minister's Office. His fame spread further and he was invited to the Russian Embassy in Washington DC and met former US President Bill Clinton at the World Economic Forum in New York.

Passionate about the environment, Tom now works with a number of charity organizations and co-founded the SEED Water Project, which raised water awareness in schools in 27 countries. In 2004, he was appointed Director of Youth Programs at the International Water Association. The following year, in an interview, he hinted that another new Internet-based company was on the way, while he plans to complete his degree at Harvard in 2008.

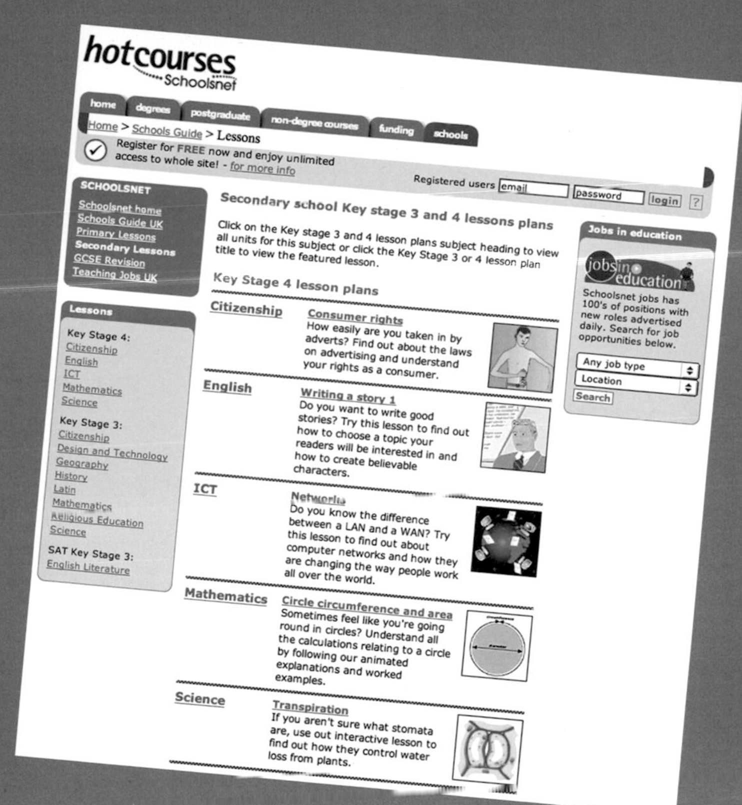

A screenshot from the Schoolsnet website started by Tom and his father.

> "I'm tremendously proud of Tom, not only because of what he continues to achieve in so many different areas. Not many young people could be so level-headed after seeing something they created as a 12-year-old become such a valuable and global phenomenon"
>
> Greg Hadfield, Tom's father, *In the Beginning* by Phil Holland on ESPN Soccernet, 2005.

weblinks

For more information about Tom Hadfield, go to

www.waylinks.co.uk/21CentLives/Millionaires

J. K. Rowling

Bestselling Author

J.K. Rowling attends the 2006 British Book Awards.

"Read as much as you can, I think that there is nothing as important, because that will really show you what makes good writing in your opinion...You probably will not like 90 per cent of what you write, one day you write a single page you like and build on that."

J.K. Rowling when asked what is the most valuable piece of advice she could give to a budding writer, CBBC Newsround, 18 July 2005

Name: Joanne Rowling

Year and place of birth: 1965, Yate, South Gloucester, UK

Education: After gaining three A-Levels in French, German and English, Jo went to Exeter University to study French and Classics, receiving a second-class degree.

Estimated wealth: £520 million

Career highs: Jo's first novel, *Harry Potter and the Philosopher's Stone*, was turned into a film in 2001 and took over £500 million at the box office worldwide. Jo's sixth novel, *Harry Potter and the Half-Blood Prince*, became the United States' best-selling book of 2005, with over 7.2 million copies sold. In 2006, Jo was voted the UK's greatest living author in a poll by *The Book Magazine*.

Away from work: Reading, writing and looking after her three children occupies most of Jo's time. She enjoys travelling and relaxing in the Scottish countryside.

Something you might not know about her: J.K. Rowling does not legally have a middle name. The K in J.K. is short for Kathleen, Jo's grandmother. The publishers suggested that she used initials on the cover of the first Harry Potter book as they were worried that boys wouldn't read a story written by a woman.

Make a million: Jo not only came up with an interesting and original idea for a story, she worked incredibly hard at turning it into a full, rich world with strong characters. This involved years of careful planning and many re-writes before her first book was complete. She also didn't give up when a number of publishers turned her down.

Rabbit – a story of a rabbit with measles – was the first story Joanne Rowling wrote. She was six years old at the time. Nineteen years later (1990), the idea of a boy wizard popped into her head while she sat on a train. It was seven more years before her first book, *Harry Potter and the Philosopher's Stone*, was published. By 2006, with six Harry Potter novels on sale, Jo had earned the status of the most famous living children's author.

A Finnish bookstore is swamped with customers keen to buy the fifth Harry Potter novel.

After leaving university, Jo worked as a research assistant for Amnesty International and did secretarial work in Manchester. In 1991, the year after the death of her mother, she headed off to Portugal to teach English. She met and married a Portuguese journalist and the pair had a child, Jessica, before they divorced and Jo returned with Jessica to Britain at the end of 1993. She arrived back with a suitcase half-full of pages of Harry Potter storylines and chapters. Jo finally completed her first Harry Potter novel in 1995 using an old typewriter worth £40.

Jo was signed up by literary agent Christopher Little who managed to get the publishers Bloomsbury to pay a £10,000 advance for the first novel, which was published in 1997. She had always seen Harry Potter as a seven-book series, one title for each year Harry spends at the Hogwarts School of Witchcraft and Wizadry. Each of the next three years saw the arrival of a new Harry Potter novel and by the time the fourth was published in 2000, Jo was one of the highest earning women in the UK. The following year she was awarded an OBE (Officer of the Order of the British Empire) for services to children's literature.

In July 1999, Warner Brothers bought the rights to make films of Jo's books. Jo drove a hard bargain insisting that they were live action films, not cartoons, and used mainly British actors. The films were a huge commercial success and inspired yet more people to buy her books, which have now been translated into more than 60 languages.

In 2005, Christopher Little announced that over 300 million Harry Potter books had been sold. The money from the sales of these books, merchandise and her involvement in the four Harry Potter films so far has made Jo incredibly rich. Although very guarded about her private and financial life, she owns expensive properties in London and Edinburgh and in 2001 bought a nineteenth century Scottish mansion, Killiechassie House. She married Dr Neil Murray there in 2001. Speculation has mounted about what Jo will do once the seventh and final Potter book is published. She has hinted that other, quite different books are in the pipeline.

"She's a tough writer. She won't compromise on what she sees as being right, just in order to worry about what might frighten children."

Stephen Fry in the BBC TV show, *Harry Potter and Me*, December 2001.

weblinks

For more information about J. K. Rowling, go to
www.waylinks.co.uk/21CentLives/Millionaires

Bill Gates

Microsoft Mastermind

Bill Gates speaks at the Live 8 London charity concert in 2005.

"I believe that with great wealth comes great responsibility, a responsibility to give back to society, a responsibility to see that those resources are put to work in the best possible way to help those most in need."

BBC News, 16 June 2006

Name: William Henry Gates III

Year and place of birth:
1955, Seattle, USA

Education: After scoring 1590 out of 1600 in his SAT tests at school (an extremely high score), Bill was able to enroll at the prestigious Harvard University in 1973. He studied Computer Science there before dropping out in his third year.

Estimated wealth: US$50,000 million (£27,800 million)

Career highs: Bill has established Microsoft as the world's biggest computer company. He created the Windows family of operating systems for computers. He was rated the world's richest person by business magazine *Forbes* for twelve years in a row.

Away from work: Bill plays golf and the card game bridge. He has even played at the World Bridge Championship.

Something you might not know about him: In 2004, the BBC reported that Bill Gates was probably the most emailed person in the world, receiving a staggering 4 million emails each day. Microsoft runs an entire department to filter out unwanted messages to him.

Make a million: Bill rates timing and luck as two of his biggest secrets to success. Microsoft often aren't the first company to enter an area of business. They check-out competitors' products thoroughly before creating their own.

Born into a wealthy family, Bill Gates declared he would make a million himself by the time he was 20. He was not far wrong. While at Lakeside School, Bill became fascinated by computers. He and a few other Lakeside students were asked by the Computer Center Corporation to check its system for bugs and weaknesses and, in return, they received free computing time. He hooked up with another Lakeside pupil, Paul Allen, and the pair began writing and selling computer programmes.

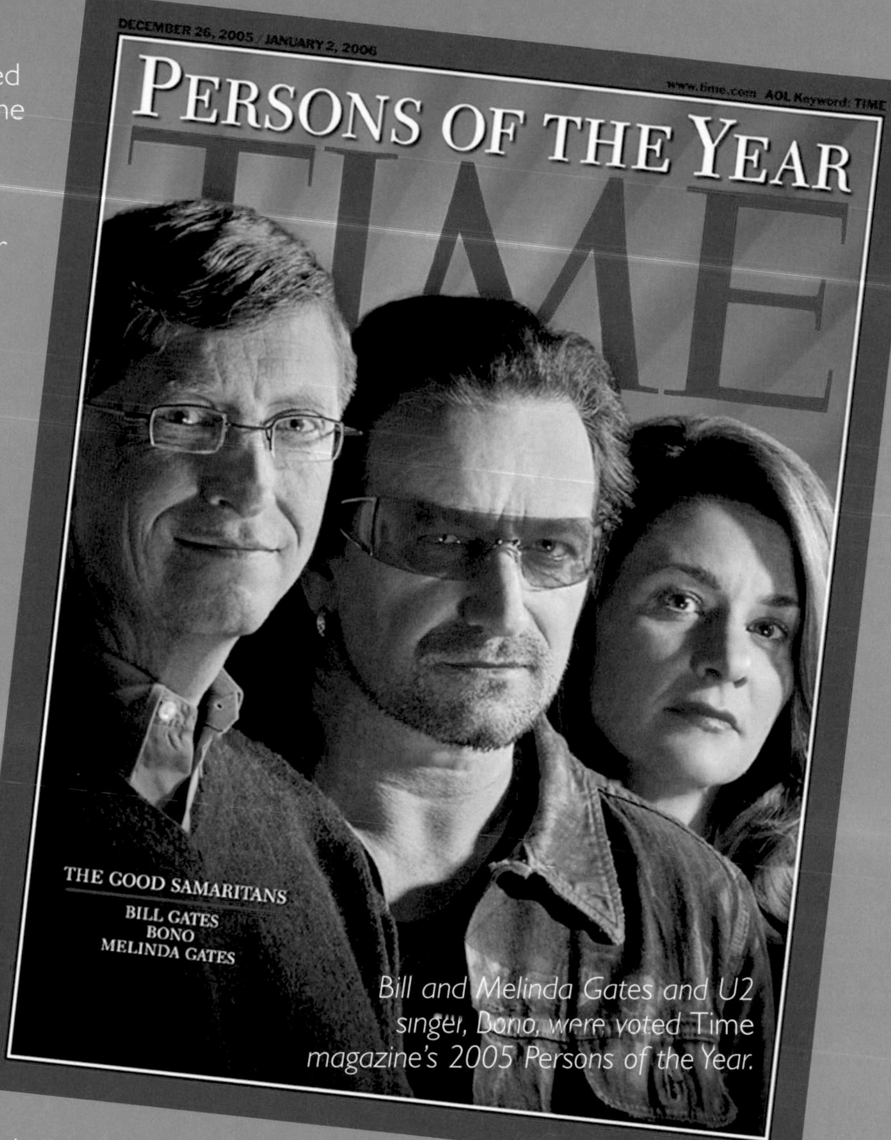

Bill and Melinda Gates and U2 singer, Bono, were voted Time magazine's 2005 Persons of the Year.

Bill and Paul moved to New Mexico and started Micro-soft (they dropped the hyphen four years later) in 1975. The company's first five clients went bankrupt but they struggled on, moving to Seattle in 1979. That was until Bill spent arguably the most profitable US$50,000 in computing history. For that sum, he purchased a computer operating system called QDOS (Quick and Dirty Operating System) from another company and eventually renamed it MS-DOS. They licensed it to the giant computing company IBM and received a small fee for every personal computer (PC) IBM sold. As IBM's computers raced off the shelves in their hundreds of thousands, the fees amounted to millions.

Building on this success, Microsoft produced famous computer software like Word, Office and Excel. In 1987, Microsoft created its first version of its Windows operating system, which, by the start of the 1990s, was selling at a rate of a million a month. Microsoft operating systems are found on over 75% of the world's hundreds of millions of computers – a prime reason for Gates' fortune. Microsoft now employs over 60,000 people in 102 different countries.

Bill married Melinda French in 1994 and they have three children, Jennifer, Rory and Phoebe. They live on the shores of Lake Washington in the US in a luxury house with its own cinema, boathouse, library, swimming pool and trampoline room. Bill is estimated to have given away around a third of his total wealth to charity. Much of this has been through the Bill and Melinda Gates Foundation, which is believed to have assets of over US$29,200 million (£15,000 million). Bill and Melinda were voted *Time* magazine's Persons of the Year in 2005 and he was also given an honorary knighthood by the Queen the same year. In 2006, Bill Gates stunned the world with the announcement that he was to step down from the day-to-day running of Microsoft in 2008 with the intention of devoting more time to charitable projects.

"I admire Bill Gates enormously. I know him individually, and I think he's incredible in business."

Billionaire businessman Warren Buffett

weblinks

For more information about Bill Gates, go to

www.waylinks.co.uk/21CentLives/Millionaires

Ajaz Ahmed

Advertising Guru

Founder of AKQA Ajaz Ahmed.

"I think that people judge you for the contribution you make, rather than your age. It's interesting that people seem more interested in my age today, actually more than ever, even more so than they did when I first co-founded AKQA. I'm actually not that young anymore, but it's still something that interests people which I find pretty fascinating."

Interview on MyVillage website

Name: Ajaz Ahmed

Year and place of birth: 1973, Taplow, Berkshire, UK

Education: After passing four A-Levels in English, Business Studies, Law and Communication Studies, Ajaz went to Bath University to study Business. He dropped out of university in 1994 and formed his company, AKQA, the following year.

Estimated wealth: £35 million

Career highs: Ajaz turned AKQA from a starter company to a global corporation employing 450 people by 2006. Nike, Microsoft and Coca-Cola are all long-running clients. Nike has been an AKQA client since 1999 and Microsoft since 1998. AKQA was named 'Agency of the Year' in the USA and the UK in 2006. It is the first company to hold the title of 'Agency of the Year' on both sides of the Atlantic, at the same time.

Away from work: Ajaz is an Arsenal fan and likes going to games when he can. He also enjoys playing football, golf, swimming and snowboarding. He loves reading and has a huge collection of books.

Something you might not know about him: When Ajaz was 14 years old he would send in ideas to companies he liked. Two advertising agencies offered Ajaz a job while he was still at school and another idea sent to watchmakers, Swatch, was turned into a television commercial. Ajaz still wears a Swatch watch today!

Make a million: "If you set out with the goal of making a million the chances are that you won't. If you set out with the goal of doing something you love to do, then it may be worth a million and you might make one at the same time." Author's interview with Ajaz, June 2006.

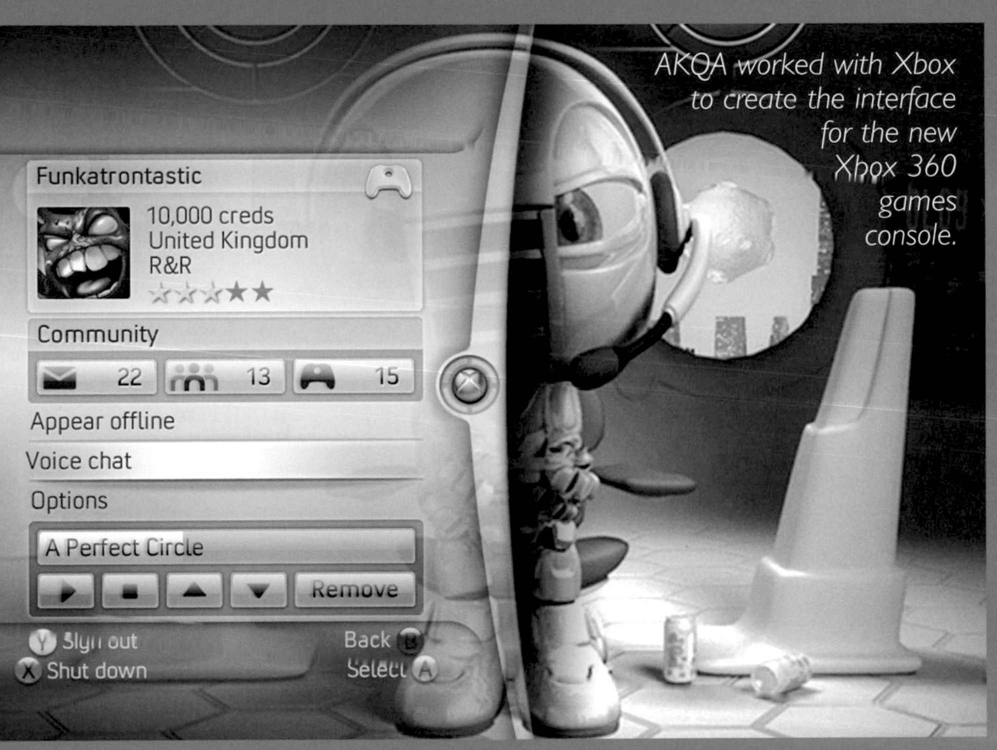

AKQA worked with Xbox to create the interface for the new Xbox 360 games console.

San Francisco, Washington DC and in 2005, New York. Although several companies have attempted to buy and take over AKQA, it remains fiercely independent. Ajaz is AKQA's biggest shareholder making him a millionaire many times over while still in his twenties.

Ajaz received an honorary doctorate in 2002 from Oxford Brookes University. The following year, he returned to Oxford, as a mentor for students at Oxford University's Said Business School. His company motto is: *The future inspires us. We work to inspire.* The company supports a number of charities for young people including the Prince's Trust, the NSPCC and the Save the Children Fund.

Ajaz Ahmed is head of AKQA, one of the most exciting and respected advertising, marketing and digital media agencies in the world. He enjoyed a happy childhood with his parents, Khowaj and Sughran, brother, Ilyas, and two sisters, Tubasim and Tasleem, in Berkshire. He was always interested in new technology and communications so it was no surprise to his parents that he started work at the computing company Apple, aged 18. Ajaz worked in Apple's marketing department but spent his wages wisely, investing in company shares. After starting his business degree, Ajaz dropped out of Bath University and in October 1995 set up a company with three of his friends: James Hilton, Matthew Treagus and Dan Norris-Jones. The company was called AKQA and it worked using the Internet and new technology for e-commerce, design and marketing.

Right from the start, the company aimed high, paying for full-page adverts in the press and producing two publications, *Netiquette* and *Successful Marketing on the Internet*. These books attracted interest from what would turn out to be AKQA and Ajaz's first customer, Coca-Cola. Other major clients began to flood in, impressed with the technical and design skills and the imaginative ideas of Ajaz's team. The agency flourished, winning many awards and gaining important clients, including BMW, Microsoft, ITV, Virgin and Sainsbury's. In 2001, AKQA opened offices in Singapore,

The future will involve more work for global clients with Ajaz looking to open offices in China and Japan in 2007. He is excited about the future and said in a 2006 interview with *Computer Arts* magazine: "Some people wait for the future to arrive and some people just go out and build it. Hopefully we'll be firmly in the second category. There are more risks involved, but it's also exciting and that excitement is what's giving the world a new lease of life."

"Ajaz Ahmed, founder and MD of AKQA, which has continually stood head and shoulders above other agencies by setting the most breathtaking creative, client management and executional standards on the Web."

David McCallum, the managing director of eBay, when asked by *Internet* magazine in 2002 who was his Internet hero.

weblinks

For more information about Ajaz Ahmed, go to
www.waylinks.co.uk/21CentLives/Millionaires

Richard Branson

Maverick Businessman

A typically cheerful Richard Branson shares a joke with journalists at a New York press conference.

"The amount of time that people waste on failures, rather than putting that energy into another project, always amazes me. I have fun running the Virgin businesses, so a setback is never a bad experience, just a learning curve."

Interview answer on Virgin.com, 2006

Name: Richard Charles Nicholas Branson

Year and place of birth: 1950, Surrey, UK

Education: After being expelled from Cliff View House School, Richard studied at Stowe School. He was mildly dyslexic and struggled with exams. He left school at age 16 with three O-Levels.

Estimated wealth: £3,000 million

Career highs: Richard established Virgin Atlantic as a major airline business worth over £700 million. He received a knighthood from the Queen in 1999 for services to industry.

Away from work: Richard is famed as an adventurer and adrenalin junkie who has risked his life on many occasions. In 1986, his powerboat, Virgin Atlantic Challenger II, crossed the Atlantic Ocean in the fastest time ever recorded. The following year, he was in the first ever hot air balloon to cross the Atlantic Ocean.

Something you might not know about him: Richard owns his own tropical island, Necker Island in the Caribbean. He bought it in 1982 for the sum of US$300,000 (£166,000).

Make a million: As Richard shows in his action-packed life, you need energy and lots of it, to make a million in business. You also need to choose good people to have around you. Richard believes passionately in working with people he knows well and prefers to promote people from within his company. In return he values loyalty and honesty in his employees.

Branson poses for the cameras before trying to set a jet fighter speed record in South Africa in June 2006.

"Branson, I predict you will either go to prison or become a millionaire." These were the words of the headmaster of Stowe School to Richard as he left in 1967. Richard had already set up his first business, publishing a magazine, *Student*, while at school. By 1970, he had formed Virgin as a record-selling company. The following year saw Virgin struggle, but Richard made the first of many massive business gambles that would prove successful. Rather than sell the business, he gambled on opening up a series of record stores as well as starting his own record label.

The label's first release was an instrumental album by an unknown musician. *Tubular Bells* by Mike Oldfield proved to be one of the most successful albums of all time, with over 17 million copies sold. Virgin went on to sign strong-selling acts such as the Sex Pistols, Genesis and Culture Club. Richard famously wept in 1992 when he sold his record company to EMI to help keep other Virgin businesses afloat, including Virgin Airlines, which he had started in 1984.

Branson is famous for his informal work style. He rarely wears a suit and is a fun-loving practical joker. Yet, he is deadly serious about business and wants to win. He has used himself cleverly to promote his businesses and today there are over 200 of them in more than 30 countries. The Virgin brand has expanded into railways, finance, the Internet, drinks, hotels and cosmetics.

In 2005, his Virgin Mobile phone business was taken over by NTL for a cool £962 million. Business experts expect Branson to continue to buy and sell businesses in the near future. Far and away the most exciting of his future plans is the setting up of Virgin Galactic. This company aims to take around 500 tourists per year, each paying a little over £110,000, into space. Spaceports in Scotland, Sweden and the United States are being considered, while the construction of space vehicles is already under way.

"Branson's business instincts are matched by an ability to motivate people who work for him. And who wouldn't want to? Branson seems hell-bent on making sure that everybody, but everybody, is having as much fun as he is."

Time magazine reviewing his 1999 autobiography, *Losing My Virginity.*

weblinks

For more information about Richard Branson, go to **www.waylinks.co.uk/21CentLives/Millionaires**

Elle Macpherson

Supermodel Businesswoman

Elle Macpherson attends a fashion conference in Dubai in 2005.

"A celebrity name is never enough for an intelligent mass market ...truly successful businesses are born of passion and heartfelt interest."

Elle quoted in the *International Herald Tribune*, 13 September 2005

Name: Elle Macpherson

Year and place of birth: 1964, Killara, New South Wales, Australia

Education: Elle studied one year of pre-law at Sydney University before entering modelling.

Estimated wealth: £23-26 million

Career highs: Elle appeared as a model in every copy of the influential French magazine, *Elle*, for six years in a row. She has been rated as the world's richest supermodel, in part due to her lingerie business.

Away from work: Elle has always enjoyed playing sports. She is very keen on swimming, surfing and other water sports.

Something you might not know about her: Elle is hugely popular in Australia. So much so that on 21 March 1999, she became the first living Australian celebrity to be put on a postage stamp.

Make a million: Unlike many celebrities who lend their name to products, Elle does her homework. She has been actively involved in all stages of her lingerie's design, production and marketing. By promoting it herself instead of using other models, Elle gets maximum attention without her company having to pay supermodel-sized fees.

Born Eleanor Nancy Gow, Elle was the eldest of three children whose parents split up when she was 14. Sporty and into ballet when at school, she took the name of her stepfather, Neil Macpherson when her mother remarried. After her first year at university, Elle was on holiday, skiing in the American resort of Aspen, when she was discovered by a modelling agency. She left university and signed up with Chick Model Management in the United States. Work came in thick and fast, and soon she was delighting fashion designers on the catwalk and at photo shoots. Nicknamed 'The Body' by *Time* magazine in 1986, Elle appeared on the cover of *America's Sports Illustrated* swimsuit issue a record four times.

Elle was aware that the career of many models was very short and so she started to branch out into other areas. 1990 was a pivotal year for her, she made her first acting appearance with a small walk-on part in the Woody Allen film, *Alice*. Elle would go on to take larger roles in a number of movies, including *Sirens*, *Batman and Robin* and the 1997 film *Jane Eyre* alongside Oscar-winner William Hurt. She also appeared in five episodes of the popular American sitcom *Friends*. 1990 also saw her enter business for the first time, working with New Zealand underwear manufacturer Benton to create her own lingerie range known as Elle Macpherson Intimates.

Elle released a best-selling fitness video in 1994 and went into business with fellow supermodels: Naomi Campbell, Claudia Schiffer and Christy Turlington as part owner of the Fashion Café restaurant chain. The restaurants folded in 1999 but Elle Macpherson Intimates has gone from strength to strength, selling over £20 million worth of products per year. In 2005, Elle was named *Glamour* magazine's Entrepreneur of the Year, the same year that she was appointed as an ambassador for the worldwide children's charity, UNICEF. As Elle has learned more about business, her sights have grown broader. In 2004, she registered her name as a trade name for future products which may range from kitchen goods to toiletries. She has launched a range of men's underwear and is promoting the Intimates range of women's lingerie in the United States with skyscraper-high billboards. Elle's business skills were recognised by another company in July 2006 when she was invited to become an executive director of surfwear company Red Hot Tuna.

Elle poses for photos as she promotes a new range of products at a London store.

"She's the most financially astute supermodel of our times. She has turned her image into one of the most successful brand management stories. She has a terrific eye for style and trends."

Ranjit Murugason, Chairman of Red Hot Tuna, *The New Zealand Herald*, 10 July 2006.

weblinks

For more information about Elle Macpherson, go to **www.waylinks.co.uk/21CentLives/Millionaires**

Steve Jobs

Apple and Pixar Legend

Steve Jobs displays the latest generation video iPod digital player.

Name: Steven Paul Jobs

Year and place of birth: 1955, San Alto, California, USA

Education: Steve graduated from Homestead High School and registered at Reed College in Portland, Oregon to study physics, literature and poetry.

Estimated wealth: Over £2,050 million

Career highs: Steve was behind the creation of the Apple II, Apple Macintosh, and iPod electronic products, which helped make Apple a leading computing company. He transformed Pixar into a massive and popular animation company. He introduced iTunes – now the number one music download software and store.

Away from work: Steve is a passionate lover of music; his favourite artist is Bob Dylan.

Something you might not know about him: Since becoming head of Apple for a second time in 1997, Steve's official salary as CEO (Chief Executive Officer) is just one US dollar (55p) per year. However, he does get the occasional big gift from the company such as a £50 million luxury business jet in 1999.

Make a million: You must be passionate about your ideas and products in order to succeed in business. Steve has always been passionate and excited about his work and pushes everyone around him to create the very best.

> **"The only way to do great work is to love what you do. If you haven't found it yet, keep looking. Don't settle. As with all matters of the heart, you'll know when you find it."**
>
> **Excerpt of a speech given to graduates at Stanford University by Steve Jobs, June 2005**

A scene from the movie, The Incredibles: a box-office hit for Pixar.

Steve Jobs is a computing visionary who founded the Apple company as a 21-year-old with fellow computer enthusiast Steve Wozniak in 1976. The pair built their first Apple computer in Steve's parent's garage and he had to sell his camper van to raise money for the parts. Orders trickled in for their first machine, but became a flood for their second computer, The Apple II, once word got round the following year. The Apple II was the first personal computer to come with a built-in keyboard, sound and was the first PC that could produce colour graphics when connected to a colour television. At a time when home computers were extremely basic and built in their dozens, the Apple II was revolutionary and over two million were produced in a number of versions. By the mid-1980s, the first Apple Macintosh was on sale, but it was an unhappy time for Steve. After criticism about the way he managed some staff, he was ousted in a boardroom struggle. He left Apple in 1985 having sold all but one of his shares in the company.

In 1986, Steve paid ten million dollars for the computer graphics department of Lucasfilms, the company that made *Star Wars*. Renaming it Pixar, this company went on to produce some of the most popular and profitable animated films of all time, starting with *Toy Story* and including *A Bug's Life*, *Monsters Inc*, *The Incredibles* and *Cars*. The company's films have won 20 Oscars and have taken more than £1,750 million at the box office. In 2006, Pixar was bought by the Walt Disney Company for over £4,100 million. The deal made Steve even wealthier and he now owns more shares in Disney than any other individual.

Back in 1985, Steve had formed another computing company, NeXT after leaving Apple. Eleven years later, he returned home when Apple bought up NeXT. He quickly became head of Apple again and helped steer the company out of difficulties and to oversee new iMac and Apple Powerbook computers. The company received a boost from its development of the iPod digital music player, the first version of which Steve unveiled in 2001. Since that time, sales of iPods are estimated to have broken the 50 million barrier. The iTunes music store was launched in 2003 and has been an equally resounding success. On 23 February 2006, Apple announced that iTunes had sold its 1,000 millionth song. The billionth tune was *Speed of Sound* by Coldplay bought by teenager Alex Ostrovsky, who received a stack of Apple products as well as a ten thousand dollar iTunes voucher.

"He's created a remarkable legacy. I truly believe that we don't have anyone like him in our time."

Steve's friend, Roger McNamee, *Christian Science Monitor*, 31 January 2005.

weblinks

For more information about Steve Jobs, go to

www.waylinks.co.uk/21CentLives/Millionaires

Anita Roddick

Ethical Entrepreneur

Anita Roddick speaks at the launch of her new book, Take it Personally.

"Running that first shop taught me business is not financial science, it's about trading: buying and selling. It's about creating a product or service so good that people will pay for it. Now, 30 years on, the Body Shop is a multi-local business with over 2,045 stores, serving over 77 million customers, in 51 different markets, in 25 different languages and across 12 time zones. And I haven't a clue how we got here!"

Anita Roddick

Name: Dame Anita Roddick

Year and place of birth: 1942, Littlehampton, Sussex, UK

Education: Anita failed her exam to go to grammar school and went to Maude Allen Secondary Modern School. She passed a number of exams before entering Newton Park Training College in Bath to train as a teacher.

Estimated wealth: £130 million

Career highs: Anita became a millionaire in April 1984 by selling shares in the Body Shop company. She was knighted by the Queen in 2003 as Dame Anita Roddick for services to retailing, the environment and charity.

Away from work: Travel and campaigning on issues remain Anita's twin passions. She often gets the chance to combine these as she treks round the world supporting causes and seeking out new ones.

Something you might not know about her: Anita was given 24 hours to leave South Africa in the mid-1960s when the policy of apartheid, which kept white and black people in South Africa apart, was at its height. Her crime had been to go to a jazz music club that only black people were allowed to attend.

Make a million: From her experiences with her restaurant in the 1970s, Anita quickly learnt that when one idea doesn't work, you must change or move on to another idea. Experiment with different products. The Body Shop's range has grown from 15 items to more than 300.

Inside a Body Shop store in London. Roddick remains a Non-Executive Director of the company despite its sale to L'Oreal.

The daughter of Italian immigrants who ran a seaside café, Anita, or 'Bubbles' as she was known at school, was a lively, talkative child. Her powers of persuasion, along with a burning desire to do good, saw her talk her way into a secretarial job at the United Nations when she was 21. After travelling round the world in the mid-1960s, she returned to Britain and met Gordon Roddick who she married in 1970. The pair opened a hotel and a restaurant and struggled, at first, when customers did not turn up for their gourmet food. Anita and Gordon switched menus to simpler meals, like steak and chips, and business boomed.

It was in 1976 that, with Gordon away in South America, Anita opened her first Body Shop store in Brighton. It sold skin and hair-care products that were natural, contained no added chemicals and had not been tested on animals. Anita was passionate about recycling and reuse and made all the early products herself, often mixing up ingredients in her bath and handwriting the labels. As interest in the business increased, Anita and Gordon decided that instead of personally opening new stores, they would operate franchises. This meant that other people would set up the shops, sell Body Shop products and pay them a percentage of the profit.

The franchise system was successful and, by 1991, the Body Shop had an incredible 700 branches worldwide. As the Body Shop business boomed, helped by flotation on the stock exchange in 1984, Anita was able to use the stores to campaign on many human rights and environmental issues. She joined forces with organizations such as Greenpeace, Friends of the Earth and Amnesty International to publicise issues and campaign for change. Anita's outspoken ways have attracted a lot of support from the public whose interest in 'green' issues has grown. They have also occasionally attracted critics and untrue stories. In 1994, for example, Anita and Gordon succeeded in a court action against Channel 4 for a documentary that made untrue allegations about the Body Shop, including that some of their cosmetics contained animal products.

In 2006, the Body Shop was sold to the giant French cosmetics company L'Oreal for £652 million. Anita and Gordon's share from the sale was estimated at over £120 million. Still brimming full of energy, Anita has vowed to continue to campaign on a range of issues.

"Anita Roddick is more than a business person. Since she began the Body Shop she has turned the world of cosmetics upside down. She has changed the way cosmetics are sold, marketed and tested."

Rob Alcraft, author of *Anita Roddick*, 1999.

weblinks

For more information about Anita Roddick, go to

www.waylinks.co.uk/21CentLives/Millionaires

Jamie Oliver

Celebrity Superchef

Jamie Oliver at a book signing in London.

"No one's been more amazed than me. I suppose it was good timing, someone young, someone genuinely excited about food. I think because I was quite young and did look like the boy-next-door, the public really reacted to it."

Jamie Oliver, when asked about his success, Penguin Books website, 2006

Name: Jamie Trevor Oliver

Year and place of birth: 1975, Orsett, Essex, UK

Education: Jamie struggled with dyslexia at school and left at the age of 16 with only two GCSEs in Art and Geology. He then trained as a chef at Westminster Catering College and went to France to study French cooking.

Estimated wealth: £25 million

Career highs: Jamie Oliver was the star of *The Naked Chef* TV series and author of its three best-selling books. He founded the restaurant chain Fifteen.

Away from work: Apart from cooking and music, Jamie is into photography, gardening, flying kites and quad biking.

Something you might not know about him: Jamie plays the drums and at age 13, he formed a band, Scarlet Division, with school friend Leigh Haggerwood. After a brief appearance on *The Naked Chef*, the band were offered a record deal by Sony and their debut single, *Sundial*, reached number 42 in the UK charts.

Make a million: Jamie got his chance on television and he took it, but he didn't just sit back and enjoy the fame. He worked hard on new recipes, books and TV programmes to become one of the most well-known chefs in Britain.

At the age of eight, Jamie could be found in the kitchen of his parent's pub, The Cricketers, in the small Essex village of Clavering, peeling potatoes and helping out. It is there that his interest in cooking began. Although he was a lively, bright child, he didn't fare well at school but knew he wanted to be a chef and went to catering college. His first serious job was as a pastry chef at Antonio Carluccio's Neal Street Restaurant in Covent Garden, London. It was while working at his next job at the River Café that Jamie got his big break into television. A documentary was being filmed there and Jamie's cheeky, confident manner attracted attention. He was approached by a TV producer the day after the documentary was aired and soon had his own programme, *The Naked Chef*.

The idea of *The Naked Chef* was to strip cooking down to show how simple, quick meals could be made. The show and Jamie proved a huge hit, particularly with people who wouldn't normally watch food programmes, and led to three best-selling books and two series. Jamie became a major celebrity and since 2000, has been the public face of advertising for the supermarket chain Sainsbury's. He also promotes Tefal cookware in the United States and the UK.

His books, TV programmes and endorsements have made him a wealthy young man but he wanted to give something back. In 2002, he began an ambitious project to train 15 young people from disadvantaged backgrounds to become chefs in his new London restaurant, Fifteen. The highs and lows of the project made fascinating viewing in the show, *Jamie's Kitchen*. He opened a Fifteen restaurant in Amsterdam in 2004 and further Fifteen restaurants in Cornwall and Melbourne, Australia in the summer of 2006.

2005 started badly for Jamie when he was criticized for killing a lamb in Italy during the filming of his TV show, *Jamie's Great Escape*. But things improved with his new TV programme in which he was given a budget of 37p per child to feed 500 schoolchildren at Kidbrooke School in London. *Jamie's School Dinners* showed the poor quality of food used in some school canteens and led to the Feed Me Better campaign, which attracted over 270,000 signatures. It helped result in the British government pledging to spend £280 million on healthier school dinners over the next three years.

Jamie in action during his TV show Jamie's School Dinners.

"There's only one Jamie Oliver. Great to watch. Great to cook."

Delia Smith in a review of Jamie's book, *Happy Days with the Naked Chef.*

weblinks

For more information about Jamie Oliver, go to

www.waylinks.co.uk/21CentLives/Millionaires

Other Millionares

Athina Roussel
In January 2003, Athina Roussel turned 18 and became the richest teenager on the planet. She inherited a portion of her family estate (the Onassis family) believed to be worth as much as two thousand million pounds. The estate contains many homes and businesses, the luxury Metropole Palace Hotel in Monte Carlo, priceless artworks and an entire Greek island, Skorpios. Athina's mother, Christine Onassis, died when Athina was only three and for much of her life she was brought up in a five-bedroom villa in Switzerland by her father and her stepmother. Athina developed a passion for horse-riding and in 2005 married Brazilian show-jumper, Alvaro Alfonso de Miranda Neto, 12 years older than her. Their wedding was attended by 750 guests. The couple's home is a £5 million luxury property in Sao Paolo, Brazil. In 2006, Athina was in training, hoping to represent Greece in equestrian events at the 2008 Olympic Games.

Adam Afriyie
In the 2005 General Election, millionaire Adam Afriyie won the constituency of Windsor with a majority of 10,292 votes. He became the first black Conservative Party MP (Member of Parliament). Afriyie was born in Wimbledon. After gaining a degree in Agricultural Economics, he made his fortune in computing.

His company, Connect Support Services, was one of the first to repair and support computers for a fixed fee rather than charging for each job. This proved very popular, making Connect one of the fastest growing companies in the early twenty-first century from its high-tech headquarters in the London Docklands. A keen sportsman, Afriyie was captain of his university basketball team and is a regular distance runner for charity. He has also been the Governor of the London Museum and a Trustee of the Docklands Museum.

Charlotte Church
Singer Charlotte Church's first public performance was at the tender age of three and a half, singing *Ghostbusters* at a holiday camp in her native Wales. Her big break came when she was 11 and sung over the phone to the producers of a TV show. They booked her on the spot. Further TV appearances followed rapidly as people were amazed by her extraordinary singing voice. Her manager, Jonathan Shalit introduced her to the Sony Music UK Chairman who immediately signed her to a multi-album contract.

Charlotte's first album, *Voice of an Angel*, was released in 1998, when she was just 12. She became the youngest artist to have a number one hit in the classical charts as the album went double platinum in the UK. It sold a phenomenal 12 million copies and helped her break into the American record market. Charlotte made numerous American TV appearances, performing on adverts for the Ford Motor Company and in 2001, singing at the inauguration of US President George W. Bush.

Firing her manager, Shalit, led to a court battle that cost her approximately £2 million but Charlotte is still worth an estimated £7 million. It is bolstered by frequent TV appearances, concert tours and in 2005, the release of her debut pop album, *Tissues and Issues*. Four singles from the album all made the top 20 in the UK. Rarely out of the entertainment news, partly due to her relationship with Welsh rugby union player, Gavin Henson, 2006 saw her working on a new Friday night entertainment show for Channel 4.

John Frieda

John Frieda was born in 1951 into a family of hairdressers. He had wanted to become a doctor but after failing exams he became an apprentice at the fashionable hair salon, House of Leonard. He progressed through the ranks and styled many 1960s celebrities' hair including Diana Ross and Jacqueline Kennedy Onassis. John married singer, Lulu in 1976, the same year that he set up the first of his own salons with Nicki Clarke. He developed the famous Purdey cut popularised by Joanna Lumley in the TV show *The Avengers* and in 1980, began to style Lady (later, Princess) Diana Spencer's hair.

With salons in London, Paris and Los Angeles, a long list of celebrity clients and successful investments in property, John was a wealthy man in the 1980s. Yet, his earnings would rocket once he developed his own lines of hair products. His company, John Frieda Professional Hair Care Inc. was sold in 2002 to Kao for an estimated £250 million. He is still involved with the company and in 2006 was believed to be worth £180 million.

James Dyson

Millionaire inventor, James Dyson had a fantastic brainwave, but it took many years to turn it into a reality. Dyson had studied at the Royal College of Art and had already invented the ballbarrow: a wheelbarrow with a ball instead of a wheel, making it easier to move in different directions. He then had the idea of using swirling air to create a more efficient vacuum cleaner and one that did not use messy dustbags.

Between 1979 and 1984, he worked incredibly hard, producing a staggering 5,127 protoypes. He approached many leading vacuum cleaner manufacturers with his idea but they all turned him down. He chose to go into business to sell them himself. It would prove to be a brilliant move. The DC01, first launched in 1993, is the biggest-selling vacuum cleaner of all time. By 2005, Dyson vacuum cleaners accounted for one fifth of all those sold in the United States. According to the 2006 *Sunday Times* Rich List, James' estimated wealth was £1,050 million.

Simon Fuller

Born in 1960, British music manager Simon Fuller rose through the ranks of record company Chrysalis seeking out new music talent. In the mid-eighties he struck out on his own and guided Paul Hardcastle to a hit record, *19*, in 1985. Simon named his company 19 Entertainment as a result. He managed the Spice Girls in the early stages of their career when their first single, *Wannabe*, went to number one in 37 countries. He later created and promoted S Club 7 and S Club 7 Juniors.

By 2003, the artists he had managed had recorded a staggering 96 US or UK number one hits. Simon's wealth boomed almost overnight after he devised the *Pop Idol* and *American Idol* TV talent shows which have spawned new stars including Kelly Clarkson and Will Young. In March 2005, Simon sold 19 Entertainment for an estimated £100 million. The 2006 *Sunday Times* Rich List rated him as being worth £300 million.

Index

21st Century Lives

Contents of all books in the series:

Sports People 978 07502 4597 5
David Beckham
Michael Schumacher
Jonny Wilkinson
Serena Williams
Tiger Woods
Ellen MacArthur
Sachin Tendulkar
Paula Radcliffe
Roger Federer
Other Sports People

Fashion Designers 978 07502 4596 8
Stella McCartney
Donatella Versace
Vivienne Westwood
Helmut Lang
Donna Karan
John Galliano
Paul Smith
Manolo Blahnik
Alexander McQueen
Other Fashion Designers

Film Stars 978 07502 4810 5
Johnny Depp
Nicole Kidman
Halle Berry
Tom Cruise
Leonardo DiCaprio
Kate Winslet
Russell Crowe
Will Smith
Keira Knightley
Other Film Stars

Footballers 978 0 7502 5043 6
John Terry
Michael Ballack
Ronaldo
Ronaldinho
Andriy Shevchenko
Thierry Henry
Wayne Rooney
Fabio Cannavaro
Steven Gerrard
Other Footballers

Pop Stars 978 0752 4809 9
Britney Spears
Beyoncé
Jennifer Lopez
Kylie Minogue
Lemar
Jamelia
Robbie Williams
Justin Timberlake
Usher
Other Pop Stars

Millionaires 978 07502 5042 9
Tom Hadfield
J.K. Rowling
Bill Gates
Ajaz Ahmed
Richard Branson
Elle Macpherson
Steve Jobs
Anita Roddick
Jamie Oliver
Other Millionaires

Extreme Sports People 978 07502 5045 0
Katie Brown
David Belle
Ricky Carmichael
Tony Hawk
Mat Hoffman
Gisela Pulido
Kelly Slater
Tanya Streeter
Shaun White
Other Extreme Sports Stars

Pop Groups 978 0 7502 5044 3
Arctic Monkeys
Coldplay
Black Eyed Peas
Sugababes
Kaiser Chiefs
Gorillaz
McFly
Girls Aloud
Green Day
Other Pop Groups

WAYLAND